THE EQUAL SKIES

Poets Pub   1
The Phoenix Livin. ʋets Series

*

THE EQUAL SKIES

By

NORMAN MacCAIG

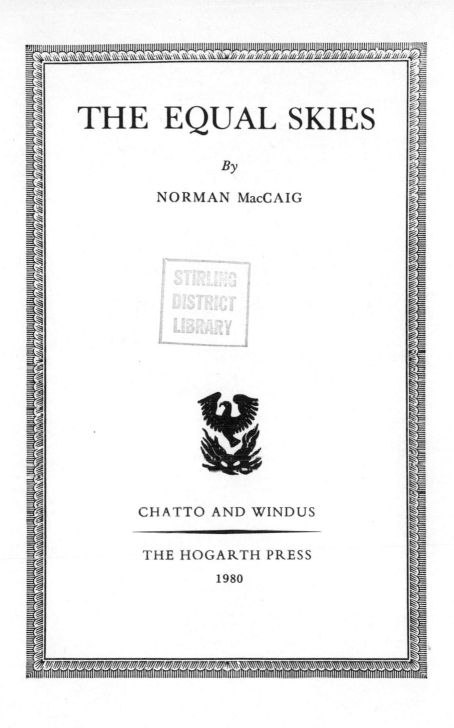

CHATTO AND WINDUS

THE HOGARTH PRESS

1980

B

2

Published by
Chatto & Windus Ltd
with The Hogarth Press Ltd
42 William IV Street
London WC2N 4DF

*

Clarke, Irwin & Co. Ltd
Toronto

*British Library Cataloguing
in Publication Data*

MacCaig, Norman
   The equal skies.
   I. Title
   821'.9'14   PR063.A15E/
   ISBN 0-7011-2491-1

8 2 1
McCA

Printed in Great Britain by
Redwood Burn Limited
Trowbridge and Esher

CONTENTS

Poems for Angus

Other Poems

POEMS FOR ANGUS

Notes on a winter journey, and a footnote

I

The snow's almost faultless. It bounces back
the sun's light but can do nothing with
those two stags, their cold noses, their yellow teeth.

2

On the loch's eye a cataract is forming.
Fistfuls of white make the telephone wires
loop after loop of snow buntings.

3

So few cars, they leave the snow snow.
I think of the horrible marzipan
in the streets of Edinburgh.

4

The hotel at Ullapool, that should be a bang of light,
is crepuscular. The bar is fireflied
with whisky glasses.

5

At Inchnadamph snow is falling. The windscreen wipers
squeak and I stare through
a segment of a circle. What more do I ever do? . . .

6

(Seventeen miles to go. I didn't know it, but when
I got there a death waited for me — that segment
shut its fan: and a blinding winter closed in.)

I went to the landscape I love best
and the man who was its meaning and added to it
met me at Ullapool.

The beautiful landscape was under snow
and was beautiful in a new way.

Next morning, the man who had greeted me
with the pleasure of pleasure
vomited blood
and died.

Crofters and fishermen and womenfolk, unable
to say any more, said,
"It's a grand day, it's a beautiful day."

And I thought, "Yes, it is."
And I thought of him lying there,
the dead centre of it all.

Highland funeral

Over the dead man's house, over his landscape
the frozen air was a scrawny psalm
I believed in, because it was pagan
as he was.

Into it the minister's voice
spread a pollution of bad beliefs.
The sanctimonious voice dwindled away
over the boring, beautiful sea.

The sea was boring, as grief is,
but beautiful, as grief is not.
Through grief's dark ugliness I saw that beauty
because he would have.

And that darkened the ugliness. . .Can the dead
help? I say so. Because, a year later,
that sanctimonious voice is silent and the pagan
landscape is sacred in a new way.

A month after his death

An accordeon and a fiddle
fit nimbly together their different natures
with such bouncing wit it makes small
the darkness outside that goes straight up
for ever and ever.

Out there are the dregs of history. Out there
mindlessness lashes the sea against the sea-wall:
and a bird flies screaming over the roof.

We laugh and we sing, but we all know we're thinking
of the one who isn't here.

The laughter and the singing are paper flowers
laid on a wet grave in an empty darkness.
For we all know we're thinking
of the one who can't be here,
not even as a ghost smiling through the black window.

Triple burden

I know I had my death in me
from the moment I yelled upside-down
in the world.

Now I have another death in me: yours.
Each is the image of the other.

To carry two deaths
is a burden for any man:
and it's a heavy knowledge that tells me
only the death I was born with
will destroy the other.

For a boat has sailed into
the sea of unknowing;
you are on board.

And somewhere another boat
rocks
by another pier.

It's waiting to take me
where I'll never know you again —
a voyage
beyond knowledge, beyond memory.

Comforter

Thank God you don't tell me
to stop thinking of him —
that I'm grieving, not for him,
but for my loss
— for, though that's true,
my grief is also
his celebration of me.

Praise of a man

He went through a company like a lamplighter —
see the dull minds, one after another,
begin to glow, to shed
a beneficent light.

He went through a company like
a knifegrinder — see the dull minds
scattering sparks of themselves,
becoming razory, becoming useful.

He went through a company
as himself. But now he's one
of the multitudinous company of the dead
where are no individuals.

The beneficent lights dim
but don't vanish. The razory edges
dull, but still cut. He's gone: but you can see
his tracks still, in the snow of the world.

From his house door

I say to myself, How he enriched my life.
And I say to myself, More than he have died,
he's not the only one.

I look at the estuary and see
a gravel bank and a glitter going through it
and the stealthy tide, black-masked,
drowning stone after stone.

Angus's dog

Black collie, do you remember yourself?

Do you remember your name was Mephistopheles,
though (as if you were only a little devil)
everyone called you Meph?

You'd chase everything — sea gulls, motor cars,
jet planes. (It's said you once set off
after a lightning flash.) Half over a rock,
you followed the salmon fly arcing
through the bronze water. You loved everything
except rabbits — though
you grinned away under the bed
when your master came home
drink taken. How you'd lay your head
on a visitor's knee and look up, so soulfully,
like George Eliot playing Sarah Bernhardt.

. . .Black Meph, how can you remember yourself
in that blank no-time, no-place where
you can't even greet your master
though he's there too?

Dead friend

How do I meet
a man who's no longer there?
How can I lament the loss
of a man who won't go away?
How can I be changed
by changelessness?

I stand in my gloomy field
like a Pictish carving
that keeps its meaning but is, too, weathered
into another one.

In memoriam

On that stormy night
a top branch broke off
on the biggest tree in my garden.

It's still up there. Though its leaves
are withered black among the green
the living branches
won't let it fall.

Defeat

What I think of him,
what I remember of him
are gifts I can't give
to anyone.

For all I can say of him
is no more
than a scribble in the margin
of a lost manuscript.

OTHER POEMS

Little Blue Blue

Are you dreaming of the big city,
of movies and bus stops and supermarkets?
Or of some girl in swirly petticoats
crossing another field with a milking pail in her hand?

Or have you been listening to the news
on the telly? — are you taking
industrial action?

Whatever way, blow your horn for me.
For my sheep are in the meadow, my cows
are trampling the brave corn flat —
and I watch them with indifference.

You look from under your feathery hat
at me dozing under a haystack
and slowly, deliciously
close your nursery eyes that rhyme with mine.

Sea change

I think of Lycidas drowned
in Milton's mind.
How elegantly he died. How languorously
he moved
in those baroque currents. No doubt
sea nymphs wavered round him
in melodious welcome.

And I think of Roddy drowned
off Stoer Point, gulping
fistfuls of salt, eyes bursting, limbs thrashing
the ponderous green. — No elegance here,
nor in the silent welcome
of conger and dogfish and crab.

Real Life Christmas Card

Robin, I watch you. You are perfect robin —
except, shouldn't you be perched on a spade handle?

Robin, you watch me. Am I perfect man — except,
shouldn't I have poison in my pocket, a gun in my hand?

I, too, am in my winter plumage, not unlike yours,
except, the red is in my breast, not on it.

You sing your robin song, I my man song. They're different,
but they mean the same: winter, territory, greed.

Will we survive, bold eyes, to pick
the seeds in the ground, the seeds in my mind?

The snow man thinks so. Look at his silly smile
slushily spilling down the scarf I gave him.

Tighnuilt — the House of the Small Stream

for Charlie Ross

In a corner of Kirkaig,
in a wild landscape, he created
a garden, a small Eden
of fruit trees, flowers and regimental
vegetables. Such labour. Such love.

It's still there, though he is not.

To remember him is to put that garden
in another place. It shines
in the desolate landscape of loss —
a small Eden, of use and of beauty.

I visit him there
between the mountains and the sea.
We sit by a small stream
that will never run dry.

Adrift

More like a raft than a boat
the world I sail on.

I say I'm not troubled — I accept
the powerful hospitality of the tides.

But I write little communications and float them off
to anywhere.

Some are Ophelias witless and singing
among the foam flowers.

But others are Orpheus lamenting
a harbour, a house there, and a girl in it.

Cormorants nesting

In this nest, newly hatched ones. Little creatures,
you're not the prettiest things in the world.

In that one, three others, each a foot long,
in one smudge of dark, downy feathers.

Bend close to that egg and you'll hear,
astonishingly, a *peep-peep* inside it. Little creature,
you're not the wisest thing in the world.

Heraldic fathers and mothers
take off and slide down a slope in the air
to the safe sea

where five seals lucently regard us. One submerges
and swims off,
its ankles tied together.

Me as traveller

The toy yacht and the clockwork liner
were bad prophets. I was to be
a bold rover? I was to carry the globe
in a stringbag of voyages?

Happy the man, I mutter,
who's had no need to travel
anywhere. I crisscross the glebe
of small Scotland and settle for
one small part of it.

America, Italy, Canada, I rested on you
briefly as a butterfly and returned
to suck the honey of Assynt
and want no more, though that honey
has three bitternesses in it, three deaths
more foreign to me
than the other side of space.

Intruder in a set scene

The way the water goes is blink blink blink.
That heap of trash was once
a swan's throne. The swans now lean their chests
against the waves that spill on Benbecula.
On the towpath a little girl
peers over the handle of the pram she's pushing.
Her mother follows her, reading a letter.

Everything is winter, everything
is a letter from another place, measuring
absence. Everything laments
the swan, drifting and dazzling on a western sealoch.

— But the little girl, five years of self-importance,
walks in her own season, not noticing
the stop-go's of water, the mouldering swan-throne,
the tears turning cold in the eyes of her mother.

No interims in history

Barbarians! growled Attila
as the pile of skulls mounted higher.
What fun! squealed Robespierre,
shaking the gloved hand of Monsieur Guillotin.
The sword of the Lord! whined Cromwell
while the church and the people in it
became a stack of fire.

It would be good to think
that Attila felt a headache coming on,
that Monsieur Guillotin fingered the crick in his neck,
that Cromwell had a grey taste on his tongue

— while, as now, the dove
flew wildly over the world
finding nowhere to land,
growing weaker and weaker.

Old Sarah

What could she live on when her husband died?

He had spent most of his last summers
lying on his elbow on a green knowe, looking
for the black-sailed ship to come into the bay.
But death put no words in his mouth — he spoke only
kindnesses and small jokes. They squeezed past
the permanent pipe in his mouth.

So what could she live on when her world dwindled to
a leaking cottage with five hens
to cluck by the rickety door? She drew
her black memories around her,
her life savings. And fed the hens.
And smoothed the blankets
in the huge dark space of the box bed.

Impatience

From its distance
the tower clock clucks twelve times
like a hen the size of Ben Nevis.

How to go on? I can no more
reach the end of this hour
than a snail can jump over a straw.

(Along the canal four young men scull
their needle of a boat, drawing a thread behind them
on the seamless garment of the water.)

I'm happy and unhappy. In my head
there's a lark singing
in a bogful of mist.

(That hawthorn smell
is a hospital room
with a man dying in it.)

Ends and beginnings —
they're seamless too.
For the tower clock
clears its throat of a dozen pigeons
and clucks
once.

I see her coming, and walk towards her
out of this trash of metaphor
into the simplicity
that explains everything.

Equilibrist

I see an adder and, a yard away,
a butterfly being gorgeous. I switch the radio
from tortures in foreign prisons
to a sonata of Schubert (that foreigner).
I crawl from the swamp of nightmare into
a glittering rainfall, a swathing of sunlight.

Noticing you can do nothing about.
It's the balancing that shakes my mind.

What my friends don't notice
is the weight of joy in my right hand
and the weight of sadness in my left.
All they see is MacCaig being upright,
easy-oasy and jocose.

I had a difficulty in being friendly
to the Lord, who gave us these burdens,
so I returned him to other people
and totter without help
among his careless inventions.

Rowan berry

I'm at ease in my crimson cluster.
The tree blazes
with clusters of cousins —
my cluster's the main one and I
am the important berry in it.

Tomorrow, or tomorrow's tomorrow,
a flock of fieldfares
will gobble our whole generation.

I'm not troubled. My seed
will be shamelessly dropped
somewhere. And in the next years
after next year, I'll be a tree
swaying and swinging
with a genealogy of berries. I'll be
that fine thing, an ancestor.
I'll spread out my branches
for the guzzling fieldfares.

The Kirk

Petitions pour into the Big House.
Haven't the people learned yet that God
is an absentee landlord?

In some Bahamas in the sky
he basks in his own sun,
reaching down through the clouds only
for the price of suffering with which to pay
a pittance to his estate workers.
In their mournful robes they patch fences
and board up the windows smashed
by theological vandals.

When he's not feeling too good, the Lord,
lounging by his infinite swimming pool, thinks
The sins of the fathers will be visited upon the children
and thanks God
that he is his own ancestor.

Bird of which feather?

All very well for hens,
sauntering about their pedestrian precincts.

But what of the ptarmigan surfacing through the snow
with a cropful of heather tips — to be mugged
by an eagle?

Or the linnet
dodging through the mountain traffic of hawks and falcons
and being arrested by a merlin
for flying too slow?

Or the tern
whose engine begins to fail
on his one-way street
from Stavanger to Stromness?. . .

And me? — I cluck and scuffle in the pedestrian precinct
of my mind. . .But is it safe? If so, why
do I keep peering into the shadowy doorways
for the white glint, the brown glare
of an elegant fox?

Highland Games

They sit on the heather slopes
and stand six deep round the rope ring.
Keepers and shepherds in their best plus-fours
who live mountains apart
exchange gossip and tall stories.
Women hand out sandwiches,
rock prams and exchange
small stories and gossip.
The Chieftain leans his English accent
on a five-foot crook and feels
one of the natives.

The rope ring is full
of strenuous metaphors.
Eight runners shoulder each other
eight times round it — a mile
against the clock that will kill them.
Little girls breasted only with medals translate
a tune that will outlast them
with formalised legs and
antler arms. High jumpers
come down to earth and,
in the centre
a waddling "heavy" tries to throw
the tree of life in one straight line.

Thank God for the bar, thank God
for the Games Night Dance — even though they end
in the long walk home
with people no longer here — with exiles and deaths —
your nearest companions.

Report to the clan

— His skin is in tatters,
he can't climb trees. He burns things
before he eats them! His face
is shiny, his feet have no toes.
Run, brothers, run
from this visitor from the past!

This was said by
the first ape that saw Darwin.

One of my difficulties

It's nice to think of things far from each other
in one mind-blink — like
a periwinkle in the sand under
whales of cloud rolling in the sky.

That's not so strange, though, as bringing the far things
together — as thinking of
Matthew Arnold keeping goal for Rangers
or Macbeth sliding a couple of bawbees
under the plate for the Wimpy waitress.

The danger is flippancy. I demand of myself
the discipline of discipline, the bible thump
of solemnity, the white yashmak
of the surgeon making the first incision.

But what can a camera do when it's peering
down the horn of a cornucopia where Catullus
skids his Honda to a halt at the door
of the heavenly Bingo hall?

I know, don't tell me. Give the camera a brain transplant
and a heart transplant. And then
to bring these two far things together. . .
That would be something, that would be something really new.

Two friends

The last word this one spoke
was my name. The last word
that one spoke
was my name.

My two friends
had never met. But when they said
that last word
they spoke to each other.

I am proud to have given them a language
of one word, a narrow space
in which, without knowing it,
they met each other at last.

Loveless love

Paulina (to give her a name) or Mary
(to give her another) — I look out from any window
and she's walking there in her white dress
(in her black dress)
and when she looks up, which she never does,
that moment becomes her eyes, which are blue,
or her eyes which are grey.

And at night when I close mine
there's a darkness which becomes
her, and she names herself
Lucy or perhaps Marybell and she names me
with a name I've forgotten or
a name I'll never have.

Being offered a Time Machine

Chat with Bonny Prince Charlie? — he'd stare at me
with wet, tartan eyes and
help himself to another swig.

Buddha? I'd be the goose
that couldn't say Bo-tree. And anyway
I can't sit in my own lap.

I could speak to Socrates, but
I'm scared of being made a fool of — my blush
would floodlight the Parthenon.

If I liked being picked up with tweezers
I could talk to Goethe;
but I don't.

Now Napoleon on Elba: we could sympathise with each other
about exile.   But in no time
I'd be recruiting cavalry.

Nero would play a tune, and I'm musical.
I'd finish up among the lampreys.

And Bach: his genius is so formidable
he'd terrify me — he'd teach me
the true meaning of fugue.

. . .It's too difficult. I'll curl up in my Timex
and be scared enough there, watching
the frightening present becoming
the frightening past.

Rag and bone

That sun ray has raced to us
at those million miles an hour.
But when it reaches the floor of the room
it creeps slower than a philosopher,
it makes a bright puddle
that alters like an amoeba,
it climbs the door
as though it were afraid it would fall.

In a few minutes it'll make this page
an assaulting dazzle. I'll pull a curtain
sideways. I'll snip
a few yards off those millions of miles
and, tailor of the universe, sit quietly
stitching my few ragged days together.

Memorials

Everywhere place names
jut up from history, carved
1314, 1066, 1939. Or last summer.

Each holds up in exhausted arms
a battle, a birth, a martyrdom. Or last summer.

The sad ones have no tears left. The happy ones
are filled with a music no one understands any more.

Last summer is beautiful and sad:
a full-rigged ship in a bottle.

I put it there. Now it sails only
in a dream of history,
tiny, ornamental and useless.

Blue tit on a string of peanuts

A cubic inch of some stars
weighs a hundred tons. — Blue tit,
who could measure the power
of your tiny spark of energy? Your hair-thin legs
(one north-east, one due west) support
a scrap of volcano, four inches
of hurricane: and, seeing me, you make the sound
of a grain of sawdust being sawn
by the minutest of saws.

Toad

Stop looking like a purse. How could a purse
squeeze under the rickety door and sit,
full of satisfaction, in a man's house?

You clamber towards me on your four corners —
one hand, one foot, one hand, one foot.

I love you for being a toad,
for crawling like a Japanese wrestler,
and for not being frightened.

I put you in my purse hand, not shutting it,
and set you down outside directly under
every star.

A jewel in your head? Toad,
you've put one in mine,
a tiny radiance in a dark place.

Fresco in my mind

The water they move in —
those angels who never listened
to the postman passing their doors again,
yet again: who never waited
while the last stranger
left the last train: those angels
who were never frantic, whose eyes never filled with tears
in supermarkets — the water they move in
is where I've translated them to.

I'm tired of seeing them pictured
perpendicular among clouds, their feet
pointing straight down from their silly nightgowns
to the world they never walked on.

Let them try now to sing
from their round mouths
while the killer whales move nearer
and they brush their sodden wings from their eyes
to look frantically for a human hand
to hoist them aboard into the clear air
of the suffering, joyful world.

Folio

To think of Gertrude as a blonde
is difficult — but peep round the arras
and see her writhing whitely on a bed
with her honest, stodgy brother-in-law.

Fortinbras is being brave somewhere
and Rosencrantz and Guildenstern are being sick
into the North Sea.

Leatherworkers are tooling and engraving
and housewives are wishing it was
the children's bedtime and that their husbands
won't come home too drunk. Lovers
look in vain for the famous cliffs.

Ophelia is troubled about her low blood count
but forces herself to go off
to her flower-arrangement class.

Shakespeare's mind, which hasn't been invented yet,
will translate all this
into gothic glooms and ghosts and garrulities. It'll omit
the leatherworkers and the housewives;
but prodigious sentences will batman on battlements
and poisonous ideas will seep through interminable corridors
to where Hamlet sits in a buzz of flies,
pretending, for Shakespeare's sake, to be fat.

Ineducable me

I don't learn much, I'm a man
of no improvements. My nose still snuffs the air
in an amateurish way. My profoundest ideas
were once toys on the floor, I love them, I've licked
most of the paint off. A whisky glass
is a rattle I don't shake. When I love
a person, a place, an object, I don't see
what there is to argue about.

I learned words, I learned words: but half of them
died for lack of exercise. And the ones I use
mostly look at me
with a look that whispers, *Liar*.

How I admire the eider duck that dives
with a neat loop and no splash
and the gannet that suddenly
harpoons the sea. — I'm a guillemot
that still dives
in the first way it thought of: poke your head under
and fly down.

Fisherman

Look at my hands —
pickled like vegetables. Look at the secret crystals
in my knee joints and shoulders. My eyelids' rims
are drawn in blood, I stare at horizons
through eyes bleached with salt other than theirs.

I step ashore on to a lurching world.
I go to a bed between waves that sails me
into the dogfish nightmare, the horror film
of crabs.

Yet somewhere mermaids, whom I don't believe in,
are supple with their combs, are supply singing,
and (though I don't believe it) the halcyon nests
bluely in a blue miracle.

Tomorrow I'll go out again — the god of the sea,
who doesn't exist, has strayed my wits —
to sail over treasures and under treasures,
and when I come back my bunched hands
will be full of things no one will see —
that the loud auctioneer
could sell to nobody.

Ends and means

The club of Hercules
wept all the time —
it didn't want
to hurt anything.

Cuchulain's spear
cursed the magic
that forced it to be
infallible.

The brain of Nero
couldn't sleep for thinking
of the ideas that Ego
formed from it.

And what about
the men in armies,
the so many men
in so many armies?

Intrusion of the human

On the tiny sea, with an archipelago of two islands,
a breeze wanders aimlessly about,
snail-trailing over mucous water, depositing
small sighs on the sand.

A day for mermaids. A day for their inhuman eyes
and voices without vibrato. Shell mirrors
keep sinking from sight.

In the kingdom of fish whole parliaments are on the move
and guerrillas lurk
in the ruins and cellars of weed.

And in the history of light a peregrine
shoots from a sea cliff. Before its moment is over
a song will have ended, a flight
stalled in a zero of the air.

An implacable scenario — till
round the skulled headland a tiny sail
loafs into view. And everything
becomes its setting. Everything shrugs together
round a blue hull and a brown sail. Everything's changed
by the human voices carelessly travelling over
the responding water, through the translated kingdoms.

Classical translation

Venus, familiar name, means
thinking of you.

I love Venus and she smiles on me
with no condescension.

She comes to me like eyes, like hair,
like breasts. She comes like laughter
and sad weeping.

The other gods move off — spluttering Mars,
manic Neptune, even Pluto — even,
to my grief, friendly Apollo.

But wise Minerva stays near.
She whispers to me the meaning
of eyes and hair and breasts. She tells me
how your laughter and your weeping
are the children of Venus
and are not to be separated.

Cock before dawn

Those dabbing hens I ferociously love
sag on their perches, half deflated.
I'll have none of it. I'm regimental. A plumbline
goes from my head to my toes. I burnish
the dark with my breast.

Lucifer's my blood brother. When I spread my wings
I'm crystal battlements and thunderbolts. I tread the earth
by pretending not to.

The West and the East are measured from me. . .
It's time I crowed. The sun will be waiting.

Genealogy

The countless generations
that have gone to produce — me.

Was the man right who said
an oak tree is just an elaborate way
of making an acorn?

But it's an acorn,
not a stone.

I say this to console myself
in my barren moods, aware
of the leafy generations above me
accepting the sun and giving it to the world
in fertile translation.

Back from holiday

Did you have good weather? they say —
meaning, Did the sun shine? was it warm?
could you see the tops of the mountains?

And I thought of the sea
scraped white by the wind, and the clouds
stampeding on their high prairies.

And I thought
of the ugly face of Socrates —
made beautiful by the grave illuminations
of the ideas behind it.

Scale

The wind was howling with a Shakespearean howling.
Leaves scuttered by in a canto of Dante.
Aeschylus lit that watchfire on a glass crag.
— But what moved us most was the glimpse we had
Of pale Catullus stealing through sidestreets.

Consequences

What you've done to me
by way of enlargements and illuminations
puzzled me till I thought of
what a kettle and an apple
did to James Watt and Sir Isaac Newton.

If you say (smilingly), "Ah,
but you're neither of these gentlemen,"
I can only reply (weakly), "Nor are you
an apple or a kettle."

What I know is, you've enlightened
my sense of gravity and raised in me
such a head of steam I'm filled
with new inventions.

My lazy bones that slept in the sun
bustle about
in an industrious revolution.
— Will you accept
my sudden discoveries, whose patent number
(they've all got the same one)
is in the telephone directory?

Puffin

Where the small burn
spreads into the sea loch
I found the mad, clever clown's beak
of a puffin.

How many times
had it whirled into its burrow
with a six-fold whisker
of tiny fishes?

How many times
had it grunted love
to its parrot-faced lover?

I clack my own beak
by my own burrow
to feel how many little fishes
I've whiskered home, and
I grunt and grunt
before whirling off again
into the huge sea spaces.

Thorns

It's usual to dislike them.
Yet what's more friendly?
What says all the time
Stay here. Don't go away?

You prune roses for the roses' sake.
They say *Glory and honour*
as they die in a blue jug.

Their incantation is no less true
than the thorn's message
— that round, red bead
on your startled thumb.

Cupid

Zen archer, plump
with your cloudy flesh,
master of disguises and sly deceiver
of house detectives

— we all know your mother
was Venus. But you keep very quiet
about your father — slippery Mercury, god
of debit and credit and inventor
of double-entry book-keeping.

When you loosed that arrow
my heart is inflamed with, see how you juggled
the rate of exchange. Fat Cupid,
I jingle my fat profits and with them
buy little presents for the lady
who, wounded by you,
gave them to me in the first place.

Earwig

You have more nicknames
than legs — some so strange, clipshears,
you'd think people give nicknames
to your nicknames.

Lord God, Saviour, Father,
your nicknames are
ingratiating flatteries.

Devil, Auld Nick, Clootie,
your nicknames
are shuddering familiarities.

I watch you, hornie-goloch,
trekking blindly across
the Gobi Desert of the floor.

Nickname the floor Life:
that's what I trek across.

But nobody ever
nicknamed me. I feel deprived.
Shall I call myself Earwig
and trek manfully on, seeking
the crumb of comfort,
the sighing, shining oasis?

Request

What I'd like for my birthday
is a box of telepathy,
a bottle of clairvoyance
and a gift of tongues.

Then I wouldn't need
to sit hunched up in my memory
staring at a screen of images
and listening to a voice
I can't converse with —
and anything I'd say
would need no translation.

— Everything would shrink
to the biggest thing of all,
the immediacy of meaning —
but with one language still to use,
the language of touch, the speechless
vocabulary of hands.

The way it goes

Reality isn't what it used to be,
I mutter gloomily
when I feel like Cortez on his peak in Darien
and then remember it wasn't Cortez at all
and feel more like him than ever.

Journeys

Travelling's fine — the stars tell me that,
and waves, and wind, and trees in the wind
tugging to go farther than their feet will let them.
Poor feet, clogged with the world.

Travelling's fine — when she's at the end of it,
or mountains breathing their vivid Esperanto,
or ideas flashing from
their always receding headlands.

There are other bad journeys, to a bitter place
I can't get to — yet. I lean towards it,
tugging to get there, and thank God
I'm clogged with the world. It grips me,
I hold it.